NEW YORK REVIEW BOOKS

POETS

EUGENE OSTASHEVSKY was born in Leningrad, grew up in Brooklyn, and is now based in Berlin and New York. His books of poetry include *The Pirate Who Does Not Know the Value of Pi* (NYRB Poets), which discusses the challenges of communication between pirates and parrots, and *The Life and Opinions of DJ Spinoza*, which examines the defects of natural and artificial languages. As a translator of avant-garde and experimental literature in Russian, he focuses on the OBERIU group (Daniil Kharms, Alexander Vvedensky) and its successors. He has received the International Poetry Prize of the City of Münster and the National Translation Award from the American Literary Translators Association.

T0036228

Eugene Ostashevsky

The Feeling Sonnets

NYRB/POETS

 NEW YORK REVIEW BOOKS *New York*

THIS IS A NEW YORK REVIEW BOOK
PUBLISHED BY THE NEW YORK REVIEW OF BOOKS
435 Hudson Street, New York, NY 10014
www.nyrb.com

Library of Congress Cataloging-in-Publication Data
Names: Ostashevsky, Eugene, author.
Title: The feeling sonnets / by Eugene Ostashevsky.
Description: New York : New York Review Books, [2022] | Series: New York
Review Books poets Identifiers: LCCN 2022015957 (print) | LCCN 2022015958
(ebook) | ISBN 9781681377025 (paperback) | ISBN 9781681377032 (ebook)
Subjects: LCGFT: Poetry.
Classification: LCC PS3565.S79 F44 2022 (print) | LCC PS3565.S79 (ebook) | DDC
811/.54—dc23/eng/20220404
LC record available at https://lccn.loc.gov/2022015957
LC ebook record available at https://lccn.loc.gov/2022015958

ISBN 978-1-68137-702-5
Available as an electronic book; ISBN 978-1-68137-703-2

Cover design by Emily Singer

Printed in the United States of America on acid-free paper.
10 9 8 7 6 5 4 3 2 1

Contents

The Feeling Sonnets   7

The Fooling Sonnets   25

Die Schreibblockade; or, The Feeding Sonnets   43

Fourteen Ways of Looking at a
     Translator; or, The Leafing Sonnets   67

Ravel Unravel   89

The Loneliness of the Hungarians   96

Albers 2   97

Notes   99
Acknowledgements   105

The Feeling Sonnets

1.

It is with profound ambivalence that we inform you of our feelings.

We read feelings as a victory of the particular over the universal.

We cannot read feelings as there are always feelings between feelings and under feelings.

If we read feelings they would be called readings. Feelings are what we feel.

Can we name feelings and do they respond to their name.

The name feeling suggests there is something to feel for here.

Does it give us hearing. Is it even here.

If it is not here is it even there.

Also if a feeling responds to a name does it correspond to the name.

Or is to respond to a name to correspond to it in part and in part to part from it.

Or is correspond what it takes two to, when not there to give one another hearing.

To give one another hearing we repeat once more with feeling.

Here are our rings taken off, here we lie to play, we play with feeling.

Where can we read if the name of the feeling we play with corresponds to the feeling.

2.

We ask if we feel the feelings that we call ours.

Feelings fork like the capillaries of a leaf in the forest.

We feel this forest is special. It is formed of numbers.

Between one tree and another there always is a third. This is why it is called forest.

As for number, is it so named because it is numb.

Between numb and numbest, there it is. Nonetheless it too is a limit.

No one has ever held or beheld a limit, uncoiled the leaf to roll out the life of its color all over the fingertips. That was a pleasing sentence.

The outlines of our feelings lie without the amens of our names.

If the numbers are real the forest is continuous.

If the forest is continuous the feeling is crowded.

If the feeling is crowded the feeling is crammed.

If the feeling is crammed the feeling is crushed.

If the feeling is crushed it touches no one.

If it touches no one there is no one feeling.

3.

It is possible to describe these hands.

You speak as if it were possible to describe these hands.

Why is it not possible to describe these hands.

What is it possible to describe. Why should these hands be an
exception.

It is possible to describe numbers. But not hands.

Numbers are numb. We have said so. But hands feel.

Hands can also be felt. Numbers cannot, not even by other numbers.

It is because numbers are numb that they can serve as objects of
description.

O hands, subjects of ascription, always my hand or your hand.

Ascriptive hands, show us what it is to feel.

Is feeling what we do on the outside or on the inside.

Is feeling what we do from the outside to the inside.

Is it what we do to the outside from the inside. Is feeling what we do.

Is feeling what we do when we do the feeling.

4.

We are trying to make sense of a feeling.

Making sense of a feeling is like building a boat from water.

Feeling is a field. It is uneven. None of its points is like any other.

A field of what. A field of being afield. Afield of what. Afield of being
a field.

Or feeling is fieldwork. For it involves an other.

When it does not involve another, it is called fooling.

Even when it does involve another, it may still be called fooling.

It never fully involves another.

To fight against fooling we think of feeling as feeling about.

Feeling about means trying to touch the object of your feeling.

It is often done in the dark. We feel about when we cannot see and
grasp.

How do we feel about each other.

We feel for each other. We feel for each other in the dark.

We feel for each other in the dark, trying to make sense of the feeling.

5.

Now is there feeling without feeling.

Take your hand. Take your hand away.

Why is a hand like a portrait. A hand is a face.

Portraits let us feel hands we must not feel. Or is it cannot.

What are we feeling when feeling without feeling.

Are we fooling feeling. Can we not take it.

What is the sign of your hand. The sign of my hand is Libra.

It is empty and swings liberally. My other hand is unbalanced.

And what is the sign of that hand. The sign of that hand is cosine.

What does it cosign. The portrait of war on the news.

It is my war by other hands. I do not feel it.

It is handy to call on war in a poem. We consign it to manipulation for
    it makes many pule.

Is a war at hand. Will it take our hands away.

On the other hand. Do we have hands for the taking.

6.

There is a you in this poem. Whose you is it.

Is it my you. Is it your you.

Is there a belonging in this poem.

Has it been left unattended.

Is belonging a possession.

Whose possession is it. Who is possessed.

Is the possessed possessed by spelling.

How do you spell you.

Or is belonging a relation.

Is belonging a relation of longing.

Is the one it belongs to the one that it longs for.

It would be you.

Must belonging end with longing.

How long is longing.

7.

Time's fool, you have a красный рот. You know what I'm saying.

Also the lipstick rubs off easily.

Your body smells like a woman's body, sometimes quite strongly.

Your pupils are like the black pearls of Madagascar. Look at how they
sit inside their oysters, that is at their desks.

A blazon is that what this is. A night watch.

Does it tell time. What does it tell time.

Stop, mighty time! For my body is falling.

I wake up in the middle of the night and my body is falling. The
Babylon of my body is falling.

My body is multilingual. It sticks out its tongues but they say the same
thing. Ah.

It signs signs. Sign, rot. Enter by gate and the inside is rot.

Unbowed towers and untoward bowers, rot. Riders on squares with
never a river, rot. Images ending pilgrimages, rot.

Dead fountains smothered with foliage.

O time's fool. I worship at all your altars. I worship at your красный
рот. *Ist das mein Rot oder dein Rot.* What are you saying.

My altars alter. My altars falter. My altars totter. My body, my body,
my body, the Babylon of my body is falling.

8.

гу
бы

гу
гу
бы

гу
гу
бы
бы

ли

One anthropologist embedded with a tribe in Brazil has argued it
    speaks a language that does not admit embedding.

In generative grammar, embedding is the process by which one clause
    is inserted inside another.

The anthropologist in question has since been disembedded from
    the tribe in question. That was the end of his fieldwork. For
    anthropologists have to be aware of the range of ways their
    activities can cause distress to others.

In economics or economic sociology, embedding refers to the degree
    to which economic activity is constrained by non-economic
    relations.

In pre-market societies economic activities are embedded in familial
    kinship, religious, and political relations.

In market societies economic activities have been rationalized, and economic action is disembedded to follow its own distinctive logic, captured in economic modeling.

9.

These are our words. What do we do with them.

We do things with them. What sort of things.

Oh all sorts of things. For example.

Feeling things.

We formulate feelings and then we feel them.

We formulate them then we feel them.

For now they have form and are somethings.

We can consequently feel them, for there is something to be felt there now.

What is to formulate. To formulate is to frame. Form is frame.

A portrait hangs in a frame. It also itself is a frame. It is a frame of a person.

A portrait does not look like a person. A person does not look like anything.

We do not know where a person begins and ends. The middle also we do not know. This is what makes a portrait pertinent.

It is the portrait that looks. By how it looks the portrait shows us how to look.

The portrait looks like a pair of glasses. A pair of glasses is formed of spectacles and a frame.

10.

We were framed. By whom.

By agents. What agents.

Agents with agency. Autonomous agents.

Their appearance was arresting.

Reading. Writing. Rhetoric. Arresting.

We gave reading a rest. We wrote.

We wrote writing. We wrote writing with rhetoric.

Our rhetoric left us. Our rhetoric left us arrested.

We were framed. We wrote what we wrote by rote.

We wrote rot. We wrote in rut. We wrote in a rut. We wrote a lot.

We wrote right and left. And left to right. Our rhetoric was arresting.

We should have known better than write words for the effect of
arresting. What do we know about arresting.

We have read about 13 x 149 and other numbers. We have read about
numbers.

Our literacy is greater than our numeracy.

11. ВЕК-ПЛАСТИЛИН

Wrote. Red. It was die Faust. The fist.

The fist with a pen. The fist with a penitentiary.

With a rotten mouth. A fistula.

A scent was sent up and rose. It was the scent of the century. When the centurions came marching in.

The fist came first. Centuries marched under the arch.

No one had anywhere to run. Instead, they greeted with roses.

LX centuries together are eligible to be read "Legion."

The centurions kept writing addresses. Look, they posted sentries at every address. Feet rose above the ground.

Here we interrupt our program. I am reading your letters.

They are blackened houses. For example A. A bombardier beetle waits for night near them.

I lie to sleep. I am shooting at tanks. I am shouting "Fire! Fire!" but they are water tanks.

I am riding a taxi to the airport. Wow was the bombing for real here. Look at all those high rises!

I am reading the Realestatepricesrose. If they match those of cities with a comparable quality of life, the war will be over.

We are the beneficiaries, the beneficiaries. We are the beneficiaries, the beneficiaries.

12.

A is for avant-garde. G is also for avant-garde. E is also for avant-garde.

E is silent. It has been silenced. It has been silenced by the avant-garde.

There is a guard in the avant-garde. It guards the E. The E has been silenced.

It is a hard guard. It bears an arm. It is possibly full of ardor.

It sits in the A. It stands in the A. It sleeps in the A.

It looks over the V. The V is a pen. There is E in it. The E has been silenced.

There is a van in the avant-garde. Is the van avant-garde. Is the van equal to the avant-garde.

Is the guard in the van. Is the van before the guard. Is the guard behind the van.

Is there E in the van. Is the van being revved. It is being revved exhaustively. There is no E in the van.

T is also in the avant-garde. Is it also silenced. It is differently silenced from E.

It is silenced differently. It is silenced guardedly. It is a T. Its silence is guarded.

13. TEACHING A POEM

Under the Pont Mirabeau cool the Seine.

A cormorant, black as a punctuation mark, comma.

The bridge is riveted. Are we riveted. We are riveted over the river.

We are riveted by rhyme.

I think of my daughters. I am here for my daughters.

My daughters are not here. Where are my daughters.

I think of Clara Smith's "Shipwrecked Blues."

 "Well I don't mind drowning but the water is so cold."

Under the Pont Mirabeau cool the Seine.

It is possible that poetry is possible but not my poetry.

I want to hold my daughters with my arms but they are not here.

Celan fell from here, arms flailing, before his time as if to Giudecca.

Dante wrote "Tolomea" but meant all the Jews of Giudecca riveted in
    ice.

My students are waiting for me to say something.

Das Lied hat gelogen. The song lied.

Sorrow was the issue. *Der Ausgang war Leid.*

Was it the sorrow of love. *War es das Leid der Liebe.*

The sorrow of love burdens not only the soul but also the body. *Das Leid der Liebe belastet nicht nur die Seele, sondern auch den Leib.*

The soul is silly. *Die Seele ist dumm.*

It is silly because it does not know how to speak. *Sie ist dumm, weil sie nicht sprechen kann.*

It is language that says things in its name. *Es ist die Sprache, die Sachen in ihrem Namen sagt.*

Actually it says words, not things. *Eigentlich sagt sie Wörter, nicht Sachen.*

Deutsch ist eine deutliche Sprache. The German language is limpid.

Sie ist bedeutungsvoll. German is full of meaning.

The meaning of "german" in English is "closely related." *Englisch heißt Englisch, weil es eng mit Deutsch verwandt ist.*

Many words in German look like many other words in German. *Viele Wörter auf Deutsch ähneln vielen anderen Wörtern auf Deutsch.*

This endows German with a light air of duplicity. *Das verleiht dem Deutschen einen leichten Touch der Doppelzüngigkeit.*

Often you write *das Leid* but read *das Lied.*

The Fooling Sonnets

15.

If Errato is the muse of poetry, who is the muse of music.

No muse is the muse of music. Any muse is the muse of music.

A muse is she musing about her meaning with music.

Take meaning away from musing and all that remains is music.

It is the music that makes for feeling and not the meaning.

Music is moving but meaning, merely amusing.

We do not mean meaning, we mean the feeling of meaning.

It is the feeling of moving and being moved. Therefore we mean to
mean meaning but we mean music.

Music names names. We assume it has meaning.

It does not mean to. It means because it names but it does not mean it.

I feel my name being called in its omen, amen, and moan. You yours.

It may be the same omen, amen, and moan. The name is not the same.

Is there a ruse in the music. How does it choose us. We are all hearing.

We are hearing. Hearing. We are not hearing. We are here.

16.

I sang of hands and unhanding, feats and defeats.

I sang sanguinely, with blood. I sang singularly. I sang singly.

My language meant languishment. In a house.

It stings that I did not sing. Enough.

I contemplate that with the indifference of a plate.

No song came near what I needed to hear.

Now that I'm a middle-aged man, O song where is thy thong.

Poetry is for children. Poetry is a poor tree and the birds are poor.

What do we want from poetry.

We want it to tell us who we are and what we think.

We want it to serve for a station of certainty, even if it's like a piece of ice in black water.

We want it to create a you. An ear.

Shouldn't an ear be also a mouth.

Yes, we want words to create a mouth.

17.

This is my totter. This is my other totter.

They play at dress and redress.

They are princesses. They wear prints. They wear prints out.

Out of what. Out of line. Out to what. Out to tatters.

They, hey. Hey do they speak.

They speak a speak. They speak a speak of mines and takes.

They speak a speak of ekes and keeps. They speak a speak of rates and tears.

They speak a speak I speak of not speaking. Hey.

My totter totters across the room. My other totter totters across the room.

My two totters totter across the room. They take a stance.

They take a stance by happenstance.

Totter, I am tot to you. I am that, other.

Totter, I am tot to you. I am that, other.

I am that other to my totters.

18.

A narrative ist ein Narrenschiff. It is a ship of fools.

Es handelt sich um Narren. It has fools all about it.

Sie segeln zwischen Narwalen. They sail narrowly.

Every Narr handles a Persian pomegranate from Persia, an anar.

Ein Narr, that is to say a jester.

The Narr narrates, the jester gestures.

He gestures gestures. He postulates postures. His postures are pastures.

He is an impostor, he writes. He writes handily.

I have put letters on the line to let them be read.

They read about behavior. Be and have make behavior.

Behavior is how you handle things. This is why it is called das
Handeln.

You give and you take. Your hand opens and your hand closes.

Your hand has five fingers. They went to the market.

They bought, sold, and ran. Now they stretch out like martyrs, each
attached to a victory palm.

19.

Daught. Daughter. Daughtest.

Thou daughtest. He dotes. She dotes.

They are doddery. They are dotards. They are doddery dotards.

The dotards in the go-carts! The daughters in the go-carts! Go, carts!

The daughters have truck in jargon. They do.

Cartwheels. They do cartwheels into sleep.

And in their sleep too. My dotty daughters.

They speak beside the point. They are radiant.

They would sleep with eyes open. To wheel into dreams better.

They keep their eyes ajar in Wilmersdorf. In Wilmersdorf of seven hills.

They placed a jar on every hill. It is a keep, a Rapunzel tower.

It may be May in Wilmersdorf. In the late light of Wilmersdorf.

Love is agape. Each leaf unfolds into a hand whose lines bespeak summer.

Love is agape. Each bird a herald jargoning the coming coming of summer.

20.

The doubters do. What.

Often it's what they want.

They do what they want as they want. Often.

Ought they. What.

It's to do what they ought that they ought.

They ought to do what they ought as they ought.

Ought they. What.

Do what they ought. As they ought.

Often.

21.

The word *daughter* is an element of basic vocabulary.

Like the word *hair*. Like the word *eye*. Like the word *ear*.

First I saw the top of her head, then her head. She made a face.

Then all of her came out.

I threw away her chocolate.

Chocolate is not an element of basic vocabulary.

It was bad to her teeth. It was making holes in them.

She hit me and scratched my arm. I felt bad.

She said she was a witch. I asked if she knew any spells.

"Yes." Proudly. "A. B. C. D..."

Spelling also makes things come out so they exist.

I exist. You exist. She exists.

The word *exist* is not an element of basic vocabulary. It came in from the outside.

But that's all right. Let us let it stay here.

22.

Berlin is green. It is made up of old growth and new growth.

A fire took place here, a conflagration.

It's called conflagration because it started with flags.

A flag is a mark. If there's a mark, there's a market.

I come from the market, make dinner, and engage in struggle.

It is a struggle to get my daughters to sleep. They sleep on bunk beds.

The bunk beds are contemporary. They come from Ikea.

They were transported by trucks. My daughters are transported.

There is a herd of unicorns on the rug below them. They come from developing markets.

In markets that are already developed, philosophers say that unicorns do not exist.

There's only one step from the remarkable to the marketable, and the unicorns have taken it.

So say the people of developing markets. But the philosophers do not hear them.

A marketing campaign at the airport says this city is *Done with walls.*

A ring of barbed wire around the airport ensures safety.

23.

My daughters fall asleep on June fourth.

How does it make sense to say "rest in peace" to the dead.

What do those words even mean, in or out of their order.

And who are you talking to, they have no ears.

My daughters fall asleep on June fourth.

They fall asleep in Berlin, also an evocative toponym.

The dead are perpetually unable to fall asleep.

How does it make sense to say the dead this or that.

How does it make sense to say they died for the future, is their future
the present present, did they give us a present.

How does it make sense, a rondeau.

Behold, the tanks have turned into factory outlets. Behold, the
bayonets have sprouted ears of corn.

The policeman's baton now conducts an orchestra. Everything turned
out for the best.

The dead stand perpetually outside the gate of heavenly peace.

24.

She is drowned already, sir, with salt water.

She was a-sailing to Lesbos with a company of her peers.

They had fled from the wars and were preparing to play suppliants.

Her town traded hands several times, being bombed by some regional
players and one—or arguably two—superpowers.

She is an evocative pronoun. A pronoun stands in the place of no one.

Let sirens sound for those who sink when a mountain summit arises
out of the sea.

They feel their way to cultural capital, for it is fitting for the feeling to
feed on the dead.

Is she drowned again in the waters of my remembrance of her? No.
After one death there is no other.

My personal pronoun is the shield of Ajax.

It is made of eight bull hides stretched taut oven a man-size,
rectangular frame.

I kill sheep in the middle of the night. O sheep, I mistook you for my
enemies.

Sir, this image shows me wading into the waters not far from the
mouth of the Hellespont.

The inscription next to my figure says *Adidas*. It is making a reference to my bathing shorts.

The water is cold, as befits a common grave.

25.

Different states.

She states. He states.

She states states. She states her states.

States she his states. He her states. She states he states.

Are they. In the state of stating. In the state of stating states.

They are in the state of stating states of stating. Develop.

Lop. Do states stay. Stay and be stated. Stay, state!

If you state you separate. Are separate states same states. You see.

They are at sea. At sea unseeingly. And or unceasingly. They do not
stay.

How bitter it is at sea. Bitter the sea. Is my bitter your bitter.

She states her bitter is better. By a bit. But better.

He is bitter. A state is a state. They are.

They are different states. How different. State.

Separate. To state is to separate. Stay unstated.

United states.

26.

The pupil is an ever-fixed mark.

It is perpetually on the lookout for its twin, whom it cannot see.

Who shall target it. What shall come out of its blackness.

What imago shall be held beheld.

The pupil is appalled by people. A is for appall.

It is perpetually on the lookout to see if the teacher is a toucher.

What does it have to tell. The pupil is pupal.

It is dumb and deserves a D. It is fixed and rooting for recess.

The pupils over your mouth are like two ocelli on the wings of a moth.

Do you know me. Have you any memory of my feelers.

We are perpetually on the lookout for bombers to resume bombing in five minutes.

We are popular. When people see me they ask: "Have you done your homework?"

I do homework and homework and homework, I have no home but I sure have homework.

Would you like to palpate my passport, would you like to peer into my pupil, dear sir or madam.

27.

What are these numbers.

They are very odd.

Are they the music of division. Is it long division.

Will there be a remainder.

What is first, number or feeling.

First is an ordinal. It is a number.

An ordinal number tells a thing's place in an order. To tell is to order.

What orders what, number or feeling. Why does this matter.

I want the feeling to be my feeling. I don't want it playing a number on me.

Numbers are the music of taking. To number is to take. Nehmen.

They are the music of naming. Face the music.

Naming is framing. Framing is claiming. It is gaming and gaining.

Book 'em, he's playing the numbers.

Book 'em, he's playing the numbers. He's pulling a number on us.

28.

It turns out that some workers are essential.

Others, however, are inessential.

Inessential workers often get more of a compensation.

It's to help them deal with inner doubt.

But essential workers are outgoing and greeted by people.

They may even put on a crown.

The crown is evidence of popularity with crowds.

Their heads are rolling, like at the end of Ancien Régime.

Essential workers in crowns resemble saints.

Virtue is its own reward and requires no compensation.

But a circle of gold helps spectators point out the saint in the painting.

Crowned heads are rolling over New York, rolling over Brownsville
and Corona.

Essential workers usually don't need that much compensation.

Virtue is its own reward and requires no compensation.

Die Schreibblockade
or, The Feeding Sonnets

For Polina Barskova

29.

I have returned to the city of my dead.

It is the living who live there. I do not know them.

The palaces have been restored and painted in pastels.

The language has been enriched with new words, such as gastropub and restopub.

I got lost on the way from the hotel to the poetry reading.

I read poems in my acquired language, the international language of commerce, science, and now the arts.

To facilitate understanding, they were projected on a screen, one line at a time.

They were afforded the attention they would not have been accorded in their home country.

It took place near a palace where my grandmother had helped at a propaganda front to facilitate international understanding. It is now a museum of Fabergé eggs.

I did not attend my grandmother's funeral because I was too far from a visa-granting facility.

I did not attend my aunt's funeral because I was too far from a visa-granting facility.

The street names have been restored to their historical forms.

The park has been restored to its historical, eighteenth-century shape.

Representations of me reading were posted on social media. I received many new friend requests.

30.

In my ahistorical childhood, I translated over snowdrifts in courtyards, past frozen garbage.

Snowdrift is *sugròb*. A *sugrob* is no drift. It is an understudy for a coffin.

Courtyard is *dvor*. Courtiers are *dvoriàne*. They study fencing.

They fence in the entrance. They fence nylons. They fence rations. They are brought rations and then they fence them. It is the rational thing to do.

Did you say language. Gauge it. What else could I have said.

I said lineage. I said garbage. I said, I translated over snowdrifts in courtyards, past frozen. Funny I thought you said sausage.

Back where I come from we had no source language. Every language in my city was a target.

They even had signs, Citizens during art activity do not eat swan from the side, it exceeds in edible cellulose (bad for memory).

But mostly languages were facilitated in the Big House. The Big House was where the courtiers played cricket. They were grilled mercilessly.

What were they grilled for. They were grilled for hours, nights, weeks, months.

Not days. Not days. Days are when cooks for sleeping. Cricket sing nighttime mostly. It has clock.

My journey to second-language acquisition took place in the
   courtyards behind the Big House. I did not know it at the time.

My source street was lacquered with many a swan. My target street
   was lined with tapestries or trellises.

At school we were schooled in courtliness, courtesy, curtness, and
   curtseys. Our chore was to choir by rote. We were the rote front.
   We acquired fronting and frontage.

31.

I died in the dark. Did you die in the dead dark.

He died in the live dark. She was carded.

We were carded by ropes. You were roped into death.

They were operated on. It was an operation.

There's an ate in operate. Eight is a figure.

A figure is a marked fig. It is singed.

It is a wilderness of monkeys. A fig is.

There was a fig without the gate. Who made it.

Out in that dark. Made it out alive.

Over ice in that dark. Taken over ice with a truck.

Was taken under ice with a truck. Who was taken how in that
    undertaking.

Who ate wallpaper. Who ate the shoes and the leather shoelaces.

Who ate the leather coats of the killers. Who ate the killers.

Nobody ate the killers. The killers ate.

32.

Ugolino city, hast du gegessen.

Schmeckt's. Wie schmeckt's, голод гелой.

Flags are flagging in Gatchina, hammers hammering down in Mga.

You fronted, you wept not without, city of Peter, you may state "dentro impetrai," I am all saltpeter within.

Who shall manumit you from the indignity of eating.

From the staining of the clothes and the chewing with the mouth open.

The body swells. Another law has taken its members.

Whose liver shall deliver you from the body of this death. Body, boding, der Boden.

Read bread. Bread. This bread is read.

Bread in double language is Brot. Das Brot.

Peter-repeater, repeat after me, poor eater: Das Brot ist zu klein. Ist das Brot oder Stein. I am not Peter.

No matter. For they shall deliver your baby by weight, and you shall say, the breadth of this bread is an hand.

Command that these stones be bred, melancholy baby, don't be blue, sprich, daß diese Steine Brot werden.

What man is there of you, whom if his baby ask bread, will he give him a stone, der ihm einen Stein biete, Peter.

33.

Peter eater bit a platter.

Bit a table. Bit a bit off.

Bit a pit out. Spat a stone.

Ate the door, empty emperor.

You first. You first. Famine before rule.

Cannons sound canons swound.

He strides, peremptory as a storm cloud.

He bought artifacts, fetuses pickled in formaldehyde, on impulse. And
still it wasn't enough.

Ate the angel, ate the steeple. Ate the gentry, ate the people.

Ate his infant son Alexis, which means wordless.

Why would you even name your son that. He forgot the name he was
going to name.

He ate and ate and ate until he was nine, and then he evacuated.

Yet if not for his pack of papers we would all be lisping in English
now.

A ruler is a thing of measurement, he induces the feral with a ferule.

34.

What word. Bread. What word bread.

Bread word *khleb*. B, read. *Kh, leb*.

B, rot. *Rot,* mouth.

Kh, breath. *Leb*, live (imperative). Cut.

B. B. B. What a B.

Bread, be. Be bread.

Be bred. Be breadth of breath.

Be dear. Bran, sawdust. Cut.

Brood. Eat bread.

Have no dread. Be not dead. Eat.

Bread is to be. Bran, sawdust. Cut.

Bread is not to be. Read.

What is read is word. Bread dear.

Word is breath. Eat word. What a beauty.

35.

Камень. Камены.

A swan engages in self-reflection.

The gardens of Leto do not commemorate Niobe.

Riven, the vernal ice drifts on the Never River.

Eva my daughter has a fever. Her face looks thinner.

She ate bread and butter my daughter.

She wants me to lie next to her, so that she may grab onto the sides of
my head and drift off to sleep.

Vater. Water.

She wakes up, goes to peepee. I hold her over the bowl.

I try to wrap her in a bathrobe. No, I'm schwitzing. I do not need it.
I'm not cold, I'm wet.

She sneezes, a Popel hanging out of her nose. *Der Popel*, but *die Pappel*.
Ich sah meine Pappel, and so on.

She "reads" Asterix and is delighted when I tell her that Ave is Eva
spelled backwards.

Papa, says Eva holding a brownish apple, schmeiss this weg. I schmeiss
it weg.

We live in Berlin.

36.

Die Siege in German is the plural of *der Sieg*, which means victory.

In French *la siège* means seat, *la chair* means flesh, and *la flèche* means arrow.

Our *siege* means you pull up a chair and wait for the city to eat through its stores and then starve, achieving victory.

The word *siege* also has a dead meaning in English in the context of dysentery.

There would have been no deaths from starvation during this siege had food stores been distributed equally.

I visited the Monument to the Heroic Defenders of Leningrad with my aunt once on Victory Day.

White poplar down was distributed equally in the air on Victory Day.

Heroic Defenders is a concept that reconciles the recipients of feasting rations and fasting rations into a single united front.

I have returned to that city famous for fronting, especially for the fronting of its façades on the river.

Now the names of its streets are restored to their historical forms, which are the forms they bore when there were stores along them (as there again are).

Now the park is restored to its historical, eighteenth-century shape.

The statue of Cronus cuddling his baby has been cleansed and now is whiter than ever in living memory.

The statues of Apollo and Artemis seem to breathe as they wield their bows, all they are missing is a statue of Niobe.

The bust "Allegory of the Transience of Life" was missing, with only the sign left on the pedestal, but now she is restored and seems entirely untouched by time's artillery.

37.

You have been renamed Letterburg. Lately and literally.

For you are a littoral city and the river rhymes around your purse.

Those who part from you place their birthplace on the tip of the
tongue, and call it their Forgettisburg address.

The deserts of your squares are speechless, the arch of your General
Staff is arch.

Letter-forgetter, letters are for climbing, die Buchstaben sind zum
klettern.

Your prospects are ladders of beech, buchene Leitern, for literature is a
beech, it is wood or wode.

This wood you call бук, read book, but in the mountains чинарь,
makar, and the letter, буква.

Fourscore and seven years ago they were holding a conversation, the
dead or die Toten.

A conversation is to be held with care, for it breaks easily.

I have broken the staff of your bread, I have broken its Buchstabe,
bookstaff, and you shall eat of it with offal and cellulose.

Beech has not much rot resistance, and is spoken of as non-durable
and open to attack from the ground with air support.

Places famous for their beech wood may also be famous for arts and
letters, for example Weimar.

Letter-forgetter, remember us in your TOT phenomenon,
Forgetterburg, vale.

38.

As a merry, can-do "poet," I mean well. I mean to tell my story.

I mean to tell my story well. My story is the story of.

My story is the story of how I got to be who I am.

A story can be desultory, predatory, or exculpatory.

As for me, my story is my history. Such is my repertory.

My history is historical, hysterical, and histrionic. Such is my inventory.

My history takes place in language. Or is it my story takes place in language.

If my story is my history then my history takes place in language. Or does it take plunge.

My language is your language. Please come in. Take the plunge.

My history has a depository of body tissue in it. Body tissue is studied under the Greek weaving term *histos*.

As a merry, can-do "poet," I am a weaver of my history. I am a we.

My history is woven of woe. If woe is its weft then whoa is its warp. It wafts on pulmonary plumage.

It has a fool, ein Tor, who minds the store. He talks torrentially but soundly. He suffers an operation and turns into a gate.

Either the gate to the repository, which is in the lavatory, or the gate to the observatory, which is two flights down.

39.

Repeating city, column after column, the pedestal rhymes with the
base, cradle of Cantor.

Cradle of Cantor, the pedestal rhymes with the base, column after
column, repeating city.

Repeating: arise, arise. From death arise, from risible death.

Ye numberless infinities, where is your witticism. Arise and speak in
ribbons with punchlines. "Behold, I suffered death by banana."
"What's a banana?"

Death by swamp water, and death by the bellowing brown river,
Pasiphaë's pacification.

Death by fire and especially death by friendly fire.

Death by state security services, because the state is always feeling
insecurity that it's not providing enough services.

Death by rationing, a rational death, when those with less food die so
that those with more food may enjoy more food.

Death by enemy, have you seen the enemy, no one has seen the enemy,
death by Goethe and Kant and Schiller, death by the Erlkönig,
death by German Romanticism.

A hydroptique death, death of the translators of Dante. A one-eyed
death, death of the translators of Homer. Death by dearth, that
is to say famine, a familiar and familial death, death of practically
everybody. Death by camping.

O you numberless infinities, grown delicate with the satieties of night soil, pull yourselves together, Osiris, is the granite keeping you down.

Be not undone, rise up and be counted, is the granite keeping you down. Rise up and return to the ranks, trade dejection for bijection, take a number and also a name, is the pomegranate keeping you down.

Trezzini. Rossi. Rastrelli. Quarenghi (our Harlequin come from Bergamo). Montferrand.

Cantor. Cantor. Cantor. A cantor in Letterburg. The cantor of Letterburg. Count. Uncountable.

40.

Shall we come together in this city. We'll meet again like lips in the syllables of its name.

Have we taken something under there. Our son.

Let's pronounce the sound of a word or maybe denounce. A byword.

Is it a silly word. Is it also a wound. Is it tightly wound. Is it unsightly.

Is it a word sung by the souls of women. We'll meet again is a song.

It emerges from their mouths like a sword. It slices open the night.

Is it sung gainfully. Is it sung soundly. Is it heard.

Is it a password. It passes. It passes controls. It passes controls unhurt.

We'll meet again in a song. We'll meet again some sunny day.

When the blue skies drive the clouds far away. We'll meet again is a song.

Is it a sung song. Is it a sun song. You will not note the sun because.

We have buried the son in sound. That we have soundly. In a shroud.

Is he unhurt. Is he unheard in a shroud of sound. Of snow.

The sound of snow. Now. We have buried him now. We have buried him.

41.

I have returned to the city of my dead.

It is my familiar. I command that it drown everybody.

Everybody drowns in tears. These are emotional tears, measuring a
    higher concentration of hormones, such as adrenocorticotropic
    hormone and leucine enkephalin, than basal or reflex tears.

The drowned lie around and consume fish oil, rich in omega-3 fatty
    acids.

It is December. In December everyone is a little bit of a Decembrist.

They follow their star in egg tempera. They back up all their contacts
    to cloud.

This way, if they lose contact, they just need to select the date they
    want to restore from, and press *restore.*

Then time will run in reverse, and all the dead shall come back for the
    restorer to be a child all over again with.

To be a child all over again is to be learning to speak all over again.
    The Russian word for language is the Turkish word for pity or
    shame.

If next time you exclaim "alas," you wish to do it in Turkish, you cry
    "yazık!"

If you address a dead person and get no reply, you can say "ne yazık,"
    which is the same as "too bad."

You who pause on the stairs, jangling the lock chain, you watch the girls in the courtyard skipping the rope of Europe.

Are these your daughters. They address each other in German.

Your guests from the future are here. May you live to watch them grow.

42. SOWJETISCHES EHRENMAL, TIERGARTEN

The hero is held.

The hero is held over a park.

The hero is held over a flame. He is held by fame.

Has he a name. No. A hero is held to be a hero.

By whom held. Whose hero.

He her hero. Because he has hose.

What hose are those. Those are some hose.

Has she no hose. No. He her hero.

Those with no hose are held. Those with hose are held.

Those with no hose are held by those with hose, then no hose.

Are they held here. They are held here and there.

They are held handily. They are held artfully.

Come up. Come up and hold my artillery.

Tank you for coming. Come again.

Fourteen Ways of Looking at a Translator
or, The Leafing Sonnets

For Uljana Wolf

43.

The aura of Laura in an aula: Laura aurea, coma, caput.

Slumbers Laura of limbs once limber, lamb amber, the balm of
Balaam.

Holy Balaam of Ladoga, land of self-reliant samovars.

Samovar, amputee, silly putty, lumber not tree, limbless Laura of no
one.

My grandfather and grandmother disembark at Balaam from a bark.

The war is over, there is an orchestra, speeches are made.

The Laestrygonian samovars pelt them with rocks from a rock over
the landing, those that still have arms, each is like a T.

The party breaks up, the orchestra hits a false note, the bark sails off
from the isle of saviors samovars.

Then poor lice come and carry the samovars off to Ultima Thule,
where they are stacked frozen like lumber.

They have lost their members, now no one remembers them.

Laurels are not for those who gave, those who saved themselves saved
themselves a membership.

Not those who go to the front, those who front are crowned with
laurels, which are for members only.

You poet are an ass who brays prays, jeder Samowar ist schrecklich, no one desires a samovar.

Everyone desires Laura who combs ihr goldenes Haar now ashen kaputt.

44.

T, pinkie. R, ring. A, middle. N, index. S, thumb.

L, thumb. A, index. T, middle. O, ring. R, pinkie.

O translator's hand, your nature is subdued to what you works in.

You are some dude or maybe some dudette. Your immersion is dire, like that of an au pair.

Philosophy begins in wonder but literature begins in ambivalence.

Where is your ambivalence, O translator? Here it is.

It is on the fence between words and words. They do not touch, being padded with felt.

It is at the crossing between words and words. They correspond by letters.

Knock, knock. Who's there? The translator. Translator, are you going postal?

They who say you do not mean what you say do not mean what they say.

How do we come to mean what we say, say we. Really.

You have to hand it to the translator. The translator is two-handed.

O translator, artist of separation, carrier of correspondence. You play a tender hand.

In the temple of nature your hand is a living hand but it is also a dyer's hand.

45.

The letter

killeth.

It killeth

later.

It killeth

by translator.

The translator killeth.

Klutz!

Keeleth... over.

Yet the letter lives

And lets to a subletter.

See you later,

translator!

See you, letter.

If a poet stands outside the subway entrance long enough, a translator is bound to emerge.

The poet was rising from the subway by escalator. Was there a translator behind the poet.

The poet and the translator are one. The publisher omitted the source text.

Stationary, the poet transferred from one train of thought to another. The translator ran for the shuttle, weaving among the people and also unweaving.

The translator lies in a trance. Does the poet possess the translator, does the translator possess the poet.

The apparition of these men and women in the subway: Is there no publisher among them.

The poet took the A, B, C at West 4th. The translator took the 1, 2, 3 at Borough Hall.

One searched for a subway station called Ithaca and found three Subways in Ithaca, while the other proceeded to Utica Avenue in search of integrity.

The poet and the translator were riding the escalator which was scaly like Geryon's back. They weighed each other with scales.

The poet found the translator wanting. The translator found the poet wanting.

To be more specific, the poet found the translator wanting the
    publisher, while the translator found the poet wanting the
    publisher.

If a poet stands outside the subway entrance long enough, the
    translator is bound to emerge from another entrance. Or exit.

The poet was rising to the surface and already saw natural light at
    the entrance, which is also the exit. The translator stood one step
    below on the escalator, holding the publisher's hand.

The poet turned around on the escalator. The translator said, I am
    going home. There is no correspondence between the words of our
    languages.

47. DIE LIST

Whoso list to hunt. Who hunts to list. So.

To drift lost like a boat at a list, for example a junk.

Like a junkie to set down the needle and then spin like a record.

The poet does not stick to the point. His twine of thought is hard to
  follow.

Why are numbers said to follow one another. Each is a plumber of
  depths.

Each lost in the sea of the arbitrarily small. Each *is* arbitrarily small.

Who can file from number to number without foundering under.

There is a ruse in the list and it makes the hunter meander.

He can't tell the hind from the fore, like somebody who has taken too
  much Ecstasy at the sex club.

His senses are deregulated… his entire agency is neoliberal!

He's transported, that is to say translated, that is to say literal only
  metaphorically but metonymically only lateral.

He squints at what it says on a collar but it's in Latin.

Something about tangerines. And it brings him around to a memory
  of the Magdalene.

How she was about to feel to see if there was another person there until being brought to order.

48.

Is the arbitrary necessary. The arbitrary is the necessary.

The necessary is arbitrary. Is it arbitrary arbitrarily.

Or by arbitration. Is there an arbiter.

There is no arbiter necessarily. There is necessarily no arbiter.

Is the arbiter among arbres and nests. Together.

They form a forest. Is the forest the same as the wood.

We would not arbitrate that. We could not agree.

We would have an arbiter. Arbitration is necessary.

There was no arbiter in the arbor. Is it the forest where we sought
harbor.

Where was the arbiter was the nail-biter. Was the arbiter in orbit.

The arbiter was in sorbet. Cast from the orbit the arbiter became a
sore arbiter.

What is the forest forecast. Would the orbiter die.

Shall we cast lots and how many. It is not necessary but lots of arbiters
would.

Lots of arbiters would not be necessary. Arbiters are outcasts.

49.

Some say poetry is already translation.

Thought worded, bordered and ordered. Incorrect.

The word is its own reward in poetry. It reigns over itself.

It is sovereign. The word is weird. It is foreign.

Poetry is when you don't understand the language.

When you don't understand, you stand under. You listen.

What you don't understand is poetry.

What you understand is translation.

Is that true. Or is it just poetry.

If it were true would it be just translation.

"The doubt that is not doubted is not the ever-fixed doubt."

I am reading a study of Laozi, which positions his lines as
    propositions.

Is there a poetry of propositions.

Is there a poetry where words don't contradict each other.

50.

The poet is entranced. The translator is enchanted.

The poet makes an entrance. What does the translator make.

Does the translator make a relation. Is it a chance relation.

Is the poet relatable. Does the translator make a difference.

The translator makes it to the beach. And the poet.

Is this what truth is. Is truth what can be related in language.

Lying at the beach can't be related in language.

Language is a sea which laps about the littoral of the world.

Does the poet enter the translator. Do they make it.

The translator enters the sea. The translator enters the sea to make pee.

The translator makes to make pee or not pee in the sea but sees seals.
    Are they carved seals.

They are sea seals. The translator chances upon them as they are
    chanting about change in the sea.

It is small change, worth not a p. It makes or takes no impression.

There is no poet on one side and there is no translator on the other.
    Between them there is no sea.

51.

Una won't clean her room but she keeps building cities in Minecraft.

When we visited Rome she said, "I would like to build it in Minecraft."

Take that, Augustus! My Augusta found Rome in brick, but she will leave it in Minecraft.

Among the green parrots of the Palatine she publicized it for all the world.

There was only one Rome, now there's more. That's amore? No, it's Minecraft.

The Forum is "ate 'em" today, for it's double the ruin with Minecraft!

The pontifex climbing the Capitol Hill with the priestess of Vesta (they do not know what to say to each other) discovers a twin brother in Minecraft. O loop-de-loop, are we to rename you "She-Wolf"?

All the sonnets ever turned out by tourists now have daughter sonnets.

"Una, get off your computer!" "But I got on only now!"

"Una, get off your computer!" "Papa, get out of my room!"

"Speaking of your room, do you have any plans to clean it?" "But I already cleaned my desk today!"

"*Where* did you clean your desk? My eyes are going bad, I can't see the clean part." "Papa, get out of my room!"

"I just hope this is not what your room looks like in Minecraft, ok?"

"Why do you even talk about Minecraft? You have no clue about it whatsoever."

52.

You are turning into Daphne who is turning into a laurel.

Except you are turning into a woman. Look, your hands are branching.

Daphne turned into a laurel with her father's help.

Your metamorphosis is more independent.

I am writing this poem in Brooklyn. I am under the sun and near the water.

You are falling asleep under the green moon of Berlin.

Buildings rise above you on both sides of the Schoeneberg-Wilmersdorf border.

Those that had been seared by bombing and those that sprouted afterwards.

You are turning as you walk by the side of the river Spree.

You are turning as you bicycle to school and from school.

You are even turning as you fight with your little sister, except you are turning in reverse then, at least mentally.

Poets and philosophers have concluded that the river Spree cannot turn back again.

Their ground was that its waters don't taste like tears.

May you be nobody's laurel.

53.

It is fall. Are we falling.

Those trees lose leaves.

That is why foliage is called foliage.

And leaves are called leaves.

O leaves. Who calls your falling.

Is it your calling. Is your calling leaving.

Is your leaving calling.

Is your coming going. Is your leaving leafing. That is, in leaf.

It is fall. Are we filing

Leaves of absence.

Are we in freefall. Do we feel it.

Are we following. That is, filing after.

Will we too be filed after

In a book.

54.

Eva advanced to a new horseback riding class.

I shall acquaint her with the thought of Gongsun Long.

Gongsun Long says a white horse is not a horse.

He denies the difference between concepts and objects.

The philosopher who says that a white horse is not a horse is not a
  philosopher.

The philosopher who says that a white horse is not a horse is a
  translator.

Translation is an art.

The articulate translator supplies the horse with an article.

Eva rides into a walled city on a white horse.

Fans with fans greet her with fanfare.

Flags proclaim "It is so hard to distinguish between concept and
  object, practically impossible."

Gongsun Long and Huizi are engrossed in a discussion concerning
  the uselessness of articles.

Nearby stands Zhuangzi rolling his eyes.

Suddenly all three of them notice Eva, set down the articles, and take
  up twirling their mustaches.

55.

There are two magpies. One flies over to the other and says.

Tell me a song. It is the song of those who are asleep in the wood.

On earth that is bones all the way down.

Do they have gold rings or gold teeth. No, it's funny.

Does anybody know why they're lost in the wood.

No, it's funny. Only the authorities who feel misunderstood.

Only the translator who left them at the mouth of the service road.

Only the guard who guards the border against disorder. He practices
in the cold behind the coils of concertina wire.

What can we find to line our nest, where we can take our rest. (That's
still the magpies singing.)

Shall their bones lie in a layer over the bones that already are in the
earth.

Sure. It's not like they'll get in the way of the next layer. Earth enough
for everybody.

It's funny, says the poet, our future is our history. How is it possible for
me to protect my daughters.

How is it possible for *them* to protect their daughters.

When they shall be returned to their countries, picked clean.

56.

Translator, transactor, transposer, go-between, in-between, matchless
  Pandar.

Make some funk in your Funkturm. Say it with me, Есть такая
  передача!

They report you transport meanings from here to there like transport.

But you ache them new. So says an old saw. Zaum is my national
  literature.

They wrinkle their foreheads, straining to recollect their past lives but
  with mixed results. "They" meaning meanings.

All they know is the moment of nonrecognition, O poor ones.

My language is not my language. This is why it is called my language.

My country is not my country. This is why it is called my country.
  Such is the meaning of their lament.

How do they deport themselves. They deport themselves nicely yet it
  cannot be said that they do not weep very much, meanings.

As you lead them on in a hermetic Stetson, O smug smuggler! This is
  the beginning of a beautiful friendship.

Gamboling gambler, unguarded gardener in the bower of
  mondegreenery—when there's no mistakes there's no takes at all.

But what would Nimrod say? And what would Wittgenstein say about
  what Nimrod would say?

Nimrod doesn't say anything as they file past because he is too traumatized by Wittgenstein's witticisms about private language: "If Nimrod could speak, no one would understand him, bwahahaha!"

So he blows that high horn, and the sound of it tells everybody exactly what he is feeling. Or does it.

Ravel Unravel

For Lucia Ronchetti

Libretto for action concert piece by Lucia Ronchetti, based on the *Piano Concerto for the Left Hand* by Maurice Ravel. Paul Wittgenstein lost his right arm in a Russian prisoner-of-war camp in World War I. Wishing to remain a practicing pianist, he commissioned one-handed piano music from the leading composers of his day. Maurice Ravel wrote his *Piano Concerto for the Left Hand* for him. When, in 1932, Ravel first heard Wittgenstein play the concerto, he hated the pianist's additions to the score. Ravel died in 1937 from an unknown brain illness that manifested itself as severe aphasia. The poem draws on writings by and about Ravel, as well as the private-language section of the *Philosophical Investigations* by Ludwig Wittgenstein, the pianist's brother.

Warum kann meine rechte Hand nicht meiner linken Geld schenken?

L. Wittgenstein

1. OUR REVELS ARE NOW OPEN

There once was a right-handed man who had no right arm. Was he a
pianist? He was a poor pianist, *ein armer Pianist*.

He lived in a concentration camp. Why? That's where people went to
concentrate in the twentieth century.

There was a concentration of campers in the concentration camp. Had
all of them lost their right arms? All of them had lost their right *to*
arms.

Only some had lost their right arms. Only others had lost their wrong
arms. All of them had lost their equilibrium.

One moment they were concentrated, the next all of them had let go.
It was just like that. It was like the falling of leaves in the month
that some parts of the Empire called Lisztopad.

It was like the game of Go. The game of Go has rules. They are
followed blindly.

Their loss had two panes, as it were, a right and a left. The right pain
the pianist knew in his lost arm. The pianist knew his lost arm was
not in pain.

The pianist also knew the left pain. It was like music he could no
longer play. Music has lures. Are they followed blindly.

2. OUR REVELS ARE NOW OPEN-ENDED

That is not right. I do not recognize my hand. Start over.

There was a right-handed man who one time did not get his hand
right. Was he a writer? He was a writer of notes.

Was he translated? His notes had no need to be translated, for there
was nothing wrong with him. The tones in his head left the notes
in his hand.

They called him a gatherer of notes, *ein Komponist*. He was composed.
He had many beautiful sleeves until the day he did not recog,
recog… Start over.

One day one noted man took eight days to compose one note. He
could not read his hand! He had to appeal to the jurisdiction of
the dictionary.

He was together until he did not know his hand. How did he not
know his hand? He did not know his hand like this.

There was an articulate man who once could not remember his hand.
He said, Hello are you my long daughters: Alexia, Apraxia,
Agraphia, Acalculia, and… what is *your* name, fair gentlewoman.
Start over.

He could not start over. He could not start over. His notes fell, it was
an emergency, *ein Notfall*.

3. OUR REVELS ARE NOW ENDED

RAVE: It is not at all like that.

WIT: I am not following you.

RAVE: That's what I am saying.

WIT: I know what I am doing.

RAVE: Know what I am doing.

WIT: I am an artist.

RAVE: Your art is to follow.

WIT: I am not following you.

RAVE: I know what I am doing.

WIT: Know what I am doing.

RAVE: I am the artist.

WIT: That's what I am saying.

RAVE: I am not following you.

WIT: Your art is to follow.

RAVE: It is not at all like that.

THE LONELINESS OF THE HUNGARIANS

Written during a lecture, in German, by a Hungarian poet that I did not entirely understand.

The Hungarians speak a language no one understands. It is said to be related to Finnish but the Finns do not understand it either. They also have an authoritarian government that was elected in honest elections. People read poems under authoritarian governments that come to power naturally, without honest elections, but under authoritarian governments that are elected in honest elections people do not read poems, because why. Thereby Hungarian poets face a dilemma. If they write their poems in Hungarian no one will understand them. Neither will Hungarians understand them, because they live under an authoritarian government they elected in honest elections, making poetry pointless, nor will non-Hungarians understand them, because Hungarian is not a language anyone understands. Therefore they write their poems in German.

For Una

Second square. Daughter square. Dot her
square. A square dot. This square is dotty.
My that is dotty. My daughter is square.
She is square with. For example, a squire.
She is square in. For example, the air. She
is square in the air. Without a scare. She is
made of a different dough. My daughter
is doughty. She doubts. She doubts her
whereabouts.About where are her where-
abouts.They are about there. They are there-
abouts. She is square in the air or there-
abouts. She laughs. Gh, gh. She laughs.

NOTES

Thank you for reading my poems. I am sorry if they are difficult. If I were a better poet, they would have been easier. My basic poetic language is American English because I spent over half my life in New York, but I also use fragments of Russian and German, because I was born in Saint Petersburg (or rather, Leningrad) and now live largely in Berlin. I thought I should annotate non-English phrases and some of the more puzzling allusions, especially from "Die Schreibblockade."

THE FEELING SONNETS

7. Красный, *kràsny,* red. Рот, *rot,* mouth (Rus.). In German, *rot,* red. The pun is Mandelstam's.
8. Губы, *gùby,* lips. Были, *bỳli,* there were.
11. Век-пластилин, plasticine century, pun on Mandelstam's век-властелин, *vek vlastelìn,* ruler century, from his "January 1, 1924." *Die Faust,* fist (Ger.). Celan's 1963 collection invoking Mandelstam is titled *Die Niemandsrose,* 'The No-one's-rose.'
13. Ll. 12-13 confuse the punishment of sinners in *Inferno* 33.126-135 with Satan entering Judas in Giotto's Scrovegni fresco that draws on Luke 22:3 and John 13:7. *Giudecca* used to be another word for 'ghetto.'
14. Казнь, *kazn',* execution; as archaism, suffering. Песнь, *pesn',* song. Mandelstam's poem on the death of Andrey Bely maintains: "often the writing says *kazn',* but the right reading is *pesn'.*" He may have been thinking of the German pair *das Leid* and *das Lied,* more alike that their Russian counterparts.

THE FOOLING SONNETS

15. Poem commissioned by Lucia Ronchetti in honor of Helga de la Motte-Haber.

17. *Totter* plays with *tot*, 'dead' in German, and 'that one over there' in Russian.

18. *Das Narrenschiff,* ship of fools (1494 satire by Sebastian Brandt). *Der Narr,* fool, jester. *Das Handeln,* action.

21. *Basic vocabulary,* the most common words of a language that refer to the most common concepts (e.g., numbers, kin, types, body parts, simple acts) and are therefore least likely to be loanwords.

23. On the thirtieth anniversary of the Tiananmen Square Massacre.

24. We were south of Troy, I bought a copy of *Twelfth Night,* and wrote this poem.

25. Jetlag in Brooklyn, a year before the 2020 election.

28. *Corona* and *Brownsville,* poorer areas of New York which, housing many *essential workers,* became the grounds zero of coronavirus in the spring of 2020.

DIE SCHREIBBLOCKADE

Die Schreibblockade, or 'writer's block' in German, deals with the siege of Leningrad in 1941-1944, also called *Blokada.* A third of the population of three million died, mostly as the direct or indirect result of famine. I wrote this cycle two years before the memory of the Blockade was befouled by the Russian siege of Mariupol and other Ukrainian cities.

29. Mandelstam's poem "Leningrad" opens with "I returned to this city, familiar to the point of tears." In 1928, the *palace* at 21 Fontanka Embankment hosted OBERIU, the avant-garde group of Alexander Vvedensky and Daniil Kharms. In the 1960s-70s the palace served as the International House of Friendship and Peace, a cultural foreign-relations organization run by the state.

30. Siege signs said: "Citizens! During artillery bombardment this side of the street is especially dangerous." *Bolshoy Dom,* or the Big House, at 4 Liteyny Prospect is the main political-police building. The penultimate line refers to Tchaikovsky and Shpalernaya streets.

31. For *fig*, see Mark 11:12-25. A fig tree figured in the evacuation of Rabbi Yochanan ben Zakkai from Jerusalem during the siege of 70 AD, or so I misremembered; rather, the fruit appeared in a nearby fragment about hunger (see the Babylonian Talmud, Gittin 56a-b, for both). I want to thank Ruby Namdar for teaching me the passages. Also see *Inferno* 25:1-3. *Leather coats*, worn by officers in the political police.

32. *Hast du gegessen? Schmeckt's? Wie schmeckt's,* Have you eaten? Was it good? How good was it? Голод, *gòlod,* hunger; together with гелой, a nonsense word, it infantilizes город герой, *gòrod geròi,* the official Soviet denomination of Leningrad as 'hero city.' Gatchina and Mga, sites of fighting on the outskirts in early September 1941. *Peter* the Great, emperor and founder of Saint Petersburg. *Dentro impetrai,* "I turned to stone within," says Ugolino to Dante in *Inferno* 33:49. The sonnet ends in an assisted collage of Leviticus 26:26 and Matthew 7:9 and 4:3 in the King James and Luther versions.

33. Peter the Great had his only son, Alexei, tortured to death.

34. This poem about Blockade bread quotes Kurt Schwitters's "What a Beauty."

35. Камень, *kàmen',* stone. Камены, *Camenae,* Roman versions of the Greek Muses. *The gardens of Leto* puns on *Lètniy sad,* the Summer Garden in Saint Petersburg. *Der Popel,* snot. *Ich sah meine Pappel,* I saw my poplar, from Celan's "Ich hörte sagen." *Schmeiss* this *weg,* throw this away.

36. Italian marble statues in the Summer Garden include those of *Cronus* and *the children of Leto.* Returning to the park as an adult, I once found an empty pedestal whose plaque said: "Allegory of the Transience of Life."

37. Poem about the 1933-1934 conversations of the circle around Kharms and Vvedensky, whose members had called themselves the *chinars* in the 1920s. *Letterburg* puns on *Leteburg,* Letheburg, Kharms's 1926 name for Leningrad. The *Arch of the General Staff* is on the Palace Square. Вук, beech, a tree called чинарь,

chinàr', in southern Russia. *TOT phenomenon,* tip-of-the-tongue phenomenon; also, *tot* is 'dead' in German.

38. *Der Tor,* fool. *Das Tor,* gate.

39. Georg *Cantor,* born in Saint Petersburg and raised there until age eleven, was arguably the greatest poet of this city of colonnades, if one imagines the most primitive operation of set theory, *bijection* or one-to-one correspondence, as the relation between the capital and the base. He proved that the set of rational numbers is *countable* but that the set of irrational numbers, being greater, is not. The penultimate line names some of the architects who built Saint Petersburg in the eighteenth and nineteenth centuries.

40. Poem mixes Mandelstam's "In Petersburg we shall converge again" with Vera Lynn's World War II hit "We'll Meet Again."

42. *Sowjetisches Ehrenmal, Tiergarten,* Soviet War Memorial in Berlin. *Der Held,* hero. *Die Hose,* pants.

FOURTEEN WAYS OF LOOKING AT A TRANSLATOR

43. *Aula,* classroom (It.). *Laura aurea, coma, caput,* golden Laura, hair, head (Lat.). *Samovars,* nickname for Soviet soldiers who lost their limbs in World War II. Often rejected by their families, they were hid by the authorities in far-off facilities, such as one on the island of *Balaam* on Lake *Ladoga.* The ending quotes from Rilke (*jeder,* every, *schrecklich,* terrifying) and Heinrich Heine's "Lorelei." I want to thank Carole Birkan-Berz for sending me *Translating Petrarch's Poetry: L'Aura del Petrarca from the Quattrocento to the 21ˢᵗ Century,* which she edited with Guillaume Coatalen and Thomas Vuong.

47. *Die List,* ruse.

55. This version of Alexander Pushkin's translation of the Scots ballad "Twa Corbies" refers to the 2021 Belarus migrant crisis.

56. *Funkturm,* radio tower (Ger.). Есть такая передача, "there is such a broadcast," from the Soviet children's program *Radio Nanny.* *Zaum* or, more correctly, *zaum',* abstract sound poetry. Nimrod, see *Inferno* 31:46–81; also *Philosophical Investigations* 243ff.

ALBERS 2

Second of two poems responding to *Homage to the Square*, a series of paintings by Josef Albers.

ACKNOWLEDGEMENTS

Drafts of these poems have appeared in *PN Review*, Granta.com, *Asymptote*, *American Poetry Review*, *Paideuma*, *Parataxe*, *Pocket Samovar*, *The Brooklyn Rail*, *Jewish Currents*, and *EuroPoe: An Anthology of 21st Century Innovative European Poetry*. Sonnets 1 through 14 came out as *The Feeling Sonnets*, a chapbook published by the Poetry Clinic. "Ravel Unravel," commissioned and set to music by Lucia Ronchetti, was included in *Three Librettos for Lucia Ronchetti*, a chapbook by Fivehundred Places. Uljana Wolf and her students translated many sonnets into German for *Schreibheft* and *Jahrbuch der Lyrik 2021*. Italian translations by Pierfrancesco La Mura were set to music by Filippo Perocco and performed by Ensemble l'Arsenale for Biennale Musica 2019. Yevgenia Belorusets translated sonnets 1 through 14 into Russian. Her Russian-Ukrainian version of sonnet 14 was posted on Colta.ru in the first days of the invasion of Ukraine. I am very grateful to everyone involved in these publications and performances. In addition, I want to thank Katja Petrowskaja, Daniel Medin, Maria Stepanova, Oya Ataman, Genya Turovskaya, Stephanie Sandler, Susanne Frank, Anita Traninger, Lyn Hejinian, Sasha Dugdale, Edwin Frank, Kevin Platt, Michael Schmidt, and Eugene Timerman for support and help with this book.

NEW YORK REVIEW BOOKS / POETS TITLES

DANTE ALIGHIERI THE NEW LIFE
Translated by Dante Gabriel Rossetti; Preface by Michael Palmer

KINGSLEY AMIS COLLECTED POEMS: 1944–1979

GUILLAUME APOLLINAIRE ZONE: SELECTED POEMS
Translated by Ron Padgett

AUSTERITY MEASURES THE NEW GREEK POETRY
Edited by Karen Van Dyck

SZILÁRD BORBÉLY BERLIN-HAMLET
Translated by Ottilie Mulzet

SZILÁRD BORBÉLY IN A BUCOLIC LAND
Translated by Ottilie Mulzet

ANDRÉ BRETON AND PHILIPPE SOUPAULT THE MAGNETIC
FIELDS
Translated by Charlotte Mandel

MARGARET CAVENDISH *Edited by Michael Robbins*

NAJWAN DARWISH EXHAUSTED ON THE CROSS
Translated by Kareem James Abu-Zeid; Foreword by Raúl Zurita

NAJWAN DARWISH NOTHING MORE TO LOSE
Translated by Kareem James Abu-Zeid

BENJAMIN FONDANE CINEPOEMS AND OTHERS
Edited by Leonard Schwartz

GLORIA GERVITZ MIGRATIONS: POEM, 1976–2020
Translated by Mark Schafer

PERE GIMFERRER *Translated by Adrian Nathan West*

W. S. GRAHAM *Selected by Michael Hofmann*

SAKUTARŌ HAGIWARA CAT TOWN
Translated by Hiroaki Sato

MICHAEL HELLER TELESCOPE: SELECTED POEMS

MIGUEL HERNÁNDEZ *Selected and translated by Don Share*

RICHARD HOWARD RH ♥ HJ AND OTHER AMERICAN WRITERS
Introduction by Timothy Donnelly

RYSZARD KRYNICKI OUR LIFE GROWS
Translated by Alissa Valles; Introduction by Adam Michnik

LOUISE LABÉ LOVE SONNETS AND ELEGIES
Translated by Richard Sieburth

LI SHANGYIN *Edited and translated by Chloe Garcia Roberts*

CLAIRE MALROUX DAYBREAK: NEW AND SELECTED POEMS
Translated by Marilyn Hacker

OSIP MANDELSTAM VORONEZH NOTEBOOKS
Translated by Andrew Davis

ARVIND KRISHNA MEHROTRA *Selected by Vidyan Ravinthiran;*
Introduction by Amit Chaudhuri

HENRI MICHAUX A CERTAIN PLUME
Translated by Richard Sieburth; Preface by Lawrence Durrell

MELISSA MONROE MEDUSA BEACH AND OTHER POEMS

JOAN MURRAY DRAFTS, FRAGMENTS, AND POEMS:
THE COMPLETE POETRY
Edited and with an introduction by Farnoosh Fathi; Preface by
John Ashbery

VIVEK NARAYANAN AFTER

SILVINA OCAMPO *Selected and translated by Jason Weiss*

EUGENE OSTASHEVSKY THE FEELING SONNETS

EUGENE OSTASHEVSKY THE PIRATE WHO DOES NOT KNOW
THE VALUE OF PI
Art by Eugene and Anne Timerman

ELISE PARTRIDGE THE IF BORDERLANDS: COLLECTED POEMS

VASKO POPA *Selected and translated by Charles Simic*

J.H. PRYNNE THE WHITE STONES
Introduction by Peter Gizzi

ALICE PAALEN RAHON SHAPESHIFTER
Translated and with an introduction by Mary Ann Caws

A.K. RAMANUJAN THE INTERIOR LANDSCAPE: CLASSICAL
TAMIL LOVE POEMS

PIERRE REVERDY *Edited by Mary Ann Caws*

DENISE RILEY SAY SOMETHING BACK & TIME LIVED, WITHOUT
ITS FLOW

ARTHUR RIMBAUD THE DRUNKEN BOAT: SELECTED WRITINGS
*Edited, translated, and with an introduction and notes by Mark
Polizzotti*

JACK SPICER AFTER LORCA
Preface by Peter Gizzi

ALEXANDER VVEDENSKY AN INVITATION FOR ME TO THINK
Translated by Eugene Ostashevsky and Matvei Yankelevich

WANG YIN A SUMMER DAY IN THE COMPANY OF GHOSTS
Translated by ndrea Lingenfelter

WALT WHITMAN DRUM-TAPS: THE COMPLETE 1865 EDITION
Edited by Lawrence Kramer

NACHOEM M. WIJNBERG *Translated by David Colmer*

ELIZABETH WILLIS ALIVE: NEW AND SELECTED POEMS

RAÚL ZURITA INRI
Translated by William Rowe; Preface by Norma Cole